The Little Handbook of DFIR

Andrea Fortuna

ISBN: 9798371735119

To all the digital forensics and incident response professionals who dedicate their time and expertise to protecting and securing our digital world, this book is dedicated to you. Your tireless efforts and dedication to your craft are what make our digital world a safer place for us all. Thank you for your tireless work and for helping to make the internet a safer place for all of us.

1. Introduction

Digital Forensics and Incident Response (DFIR) is a critical discipline in today's digital age, where data breaches and cyber attacks are becoming increasingly common. DFIR involves the use of specialized tools and techniques to examine digital devices and systems for evidence of criminal or malicious activity. It is a crucial tool for law enforcement agencies, as well as companies and organizations looking to protect their assets and reputation.

The scope of this book is to provide a comprehensive overview of DFIR, covering the basic concepts and terminology, tools and techniques, incident response process, legal considerations, and advanced topics. Through case studies and examples, we will explore how DFIR is applied in real-world scenarios and how it can help to identify and prevent cyber threats.

Whether you are a law enforcement professional, IT security specialist, or simply interested in understanding more about DFIR, this book aims to provide a solid foundation of knowledge and skills to help you navigate the complexities of digital forensics and incident response.

What is DFIR (Digital Forensics and Incident Response)?

Digital Forensics and Incident Response (DFIR) is a multidisciplinary field that combines computer science, forensic science, and law to investigate and respond to cyber crimes and incidents[1]. It involves the identification, collection, analysis, and presentation of digital evidence in the context of a criminal or civil investigation, or in response to a cyber security incident.

DFIR encompasses a wide range of activities, including:

- **Examining** computer systems and networks for evidence of cyber attacks or data breaches

- **Analyzing** mobile devices and cloud data for forensic evidence

- **Extracting, preserving,** and analyzing digital data from a variety of sources, such as hard drives, smartphones, and cloud storage

- **Identifying** and containing cyber security incidents

- **Restoring** affected systems and data

Digital forensics involves the use of specialized tools and techniques to extract and analyze digital data from a

---

[1] https://www.crowdstrike.com/cybersecurity-101/digital-forensics-and-incident-response-dfir/

variety of sources. This process requires a systematic and methodical approach to ensure the integrity and admissibility of the digital evidence in a court of law. It involves the following steps:

- **Seizure and examination**: Digital evidence is seized and examined using specialized hardware and software tools.

- **Preservation**: The digital evidence is preserved in a way that maintains its integrity and authenticity.

- **Analysis**: The digital evidence is analyzed using various techniques and tools to extract relevant data and information.

- **Presentation**: The results of the analysis are presented in a clear and concise manner, often in the form of a report or testimony.

Incident response[2], on the other hand, involves the identification and containment of a cyber security incident, as well as the restoration of affected systems and data. It is a proactive approach to prevent or minimize the impact of a cyber attack or data breach.

The incident response process typically involves the following steps:

---

[2] https://www.sans.org/digital-forensics-incident-response/

- **Preparation and planning**: Organizations should have a well-defined incident response plan in place to ensure a quick and effective response to a cyber security incident.

- **Incident detection and triage**: The incident response team should be able to quickly identify and assess the severity of a cyber security incident.

- **Response and recovery**: The incident response team should take appropriate actions to contain the incident, restore affected systems and data, and mitigate the impact.

- **Post-incident analysis and reporting**: After the incident has been contained and resolved, a thorough post-incident analysis should be conducted to identify the root cause and prevent similar incidents from occurring in the future.

DFIR plays a critical role in protecting our digital assets and maintaining the integrity and security of our online systems and data.

It is an essential tool for law enforcement agencies, companies, and organizations to investigate and respond to cyber threats and incidents. In today's digital age, the importance of DFIR cannot be overstated.

Importance of DFIR in today's digital age

Digital Forensics and Incident Response (DFIR) is a critical discipline in today's digital age, where data breaches and cyber attacks are becoming increasingly common.

DFIR involves the use of specialized tools and techniques to examine digital devices and systems for evidence of criminal or malicious activity. It is a crucial tool for law enforcement agencies, as well as companies and organizations looking to protect their assets and reputation.

One of the primary importance of DFIR is in the investigation and prosecution of cyber crimes. With the increasing reliance on digital devices and systems, the risk of cyber attacks and online crimes has also risen. DFIR professionals are trained to identify and collect digital evidence that can be used to investigate and prosecute cyber crimes, such as hacking, identity theft, and online fraud.

DFIR is also important for companies and organizations to protect their assets and reputation. Cyber attacks and data breaches can have serious consequences for businesses, including financial losses, legal liabilities, and damage to their reputation.

DFIR professionals can help organizations identify and respond to cyber threats and incidents, and take appropriate actions to contain and mitigate the impact.

In addition to its importance in investigating and responding to cyber crimes and incidents, DFIR is also essential for preserving digital evidence in civil and criminal cases.

Digital evidence can be a powerful tool in court, but it must be collected and analyzed in a way that ensures its integrity and admissibility. DFIR professionals are trained to handle and analyze digital evidence in a way that meets the legal standards for admissibility.

Finally, DFIR is also important for understanding and preventing future cyber attacks and incidents. Through the analysis of past cyber attacks and incidents, DFIR professionals can identify patterns and trends, and develop strategies to prevent similar attacks from occurring in the future.

In a nutshell

DFIR is an essential tool for protecting our digital assets, investigating and prosecuting cyber crimes, preserving digital evidence in legal cases, and preventing future cyber attacks and incidents. Its importance in today's digital age cannot be overstated.

Scope of this book

This book aims to provide a comprehensive overview of **Digital Forensics and Incident Response** (DFIR).

It covers the basic concepts and terminology, tools and techniques, incident response process, legal considerations, and advanced topics in DFIR.

Through case studies and examples, we will explore how DFIR is applied in real-world scenarios and how it can help to identify and prevent cyber threats.

In **this chapter**, we will introduce the concept of DFIR and its importance in today's digital age. We will define digital forensics and incident response, and discuss the scope of this book.

Chapter 2, will cover the basic concepts and terminology of DFIR, including digital evidence, the digital forensics process, and types of incident response.

In **Chapter 3**, we will delve into the tools and techniques used in DFIR, including hardware and software tools, data acquisition and analysis, and network forensics.

In **Chapter 4**, we will discuss the incident response process, including preparation and planning, incident detection and triage, response and recovery, and post-incident analysis and reporting.

Chapter 5, will explore the legal considerations in DFIR, including the admissibility of digital evidence in court and ethical considerations.

In **Chapter 6**, we will delve into advanced topics in DFIR, including mobile device forensics, cloud forensics, and malware analysis.

Chapter 7, will examine case studies and examples of real-world DFIR scenarios and solutions.

Finally, in **Chapter 8**, we will summarize the key points covered in this book and discuss future directions in DFIR.

2.   Basic concepts and terminology

Digital Forensics and Incident Response (DFIR) involves the use of specialized tools and techniques to examine digital devices and systems for evidence of criminal or malicious activity.

To understand the fundamental concepts and terminology of DFIR, it is important to have a basic understanding of digital evidence, the digital forensics process, and types of incident response.

In this chapter, we will define digital evidence and discuss the different types of digital evidence that can be collected and analyzed in a DFIR investigation.

We will also outline the digital forensics process, including the steps involved in collecting, preserving, analyzing, and presenting digital evidence. Finally, we will discuss the different types of incident response, including proactive, reactive, and incident response teams.

By understanding these basic concepts and terminology, you will have a solid foundation for exploring the tools and techniques used in DFIR, as well as the incident response process.

Digital evidence

Digital evidence is any type of data that can be collected and analyzed in a *Digital Forensics and Incident Response* (DFIR) investigation.

Digital evidence can be found on a variety of digital devices and systems, including computers, servers, smartphones, tablets, and cloud storage.

Digital evidence can take many forms, including:

- Emails and messages
- Photos and videos
- Documents and files
- Social media posts
- Web browsing history
- System logs and event logs
- Application data and metadata

Digital evidence can be used to investigate and prosecute a wide range of crimes, including cyber crimes, financial crimes, and crimes against persons. It can also be used in civil cases, such as contract disputes or intellectual property disputes.

In order for digital evidence to be admissible in court, it must be collected and analyzed in a way that ensures its integrity and authenticity.

This involves the use of specialized tools and techniques to extract, preserve, and analyze the digital evidence in a way that maintains its chain of custody.

Digital evidence can be a powerful tool in legal cases, but it is important to handle and analyze it in a way that meets the legal standards for admissibility. DFIR professionals are trained to handle and analyze digital evidence in a way that meets these standards.

In a nutshell

Digital evidence is any type of data that can be collected and analyzed in a DFIR investigation: it can be used to investigate and prosecute a wide range of crimes, and is a powerful tool in legal cases. However, it is important to handle and analyze digital evidence in a way that ensures its integrity and authenticity.

Digital forensics process

The digital forensics process involves the identification, collection, analysis, and presentation of digital evidence in the context of a criminal or civil investigation, or in response to a cyber security incident.

The digital forensics process typically involves the following steps:

- **Seizure and examination**: Digital evidence is seized and examined using specialized hardware and software tools. The digital evidence may be collected from a variety of sources, such as computers, servers, mobile devices, and cloud storage.

- **Preservation**: The digital evidence is preserved in a way that maintains its integrity and authenticity. This involves creating a copy of the digital evidence, often referred to as a "forensic image," and storing it in a secure location.

- **Analysis**: The digital evidence is analyzed using various techniques and tools to extract relevant data and information. This may involve examining system logs, event logs, application data, and metadata.

- **Presentation**: The results of the analysis are presented in a clear and concise manner, often in the form of a report or testimony. This may involve visualizing the data, creating timelines, and presenting the findings in a way that is easily understood by the audience.

The digital forensics process requires a high level of technical expertise and attention to detail. DFIR professionals are trained to handle and analyze digital evidence in a way that meets the legal standards for admissibility.

In a nutshell

The digital forensics process involves the identification, collection, analysis, and presentation of digital evidence in the context of a criminal or civil investigation, or in response to a cyber security incident. It is a systematic and methodical process that ensures the integrity and admissibility of the digital evidence in a court of law.

Types of incident response

Incident response refers to the process of identifying and containing a cyber security incident, as well as the restoration of affected systems and data[3].

It is a proactive approach to prevent or minimize the impact of a cyber attack or data breach.

There are three main types of incident response:

- **Proactive incident response**: Proactive incident response involves taking proactive measures to prevent or minimize the impact of a cyber attack or data breach. This may include implementing security measures, conducting regular security assessments, and training employees on cyber security best practices.

- **Reactive incident response:** Reactive incident response involves reacting to a cyber attack or data breach after it has occurred. This may involve identifying and containing the incident, restoring affected systems and data, and mitigating the impact.

- **Incident response teams:** Incident response teams are specialized groups of individuals who are trained to respond to cyber security incidents.

---

[3] https://www.ibm.com/topics/incident-response

These teams may be internal to an organization, or they may be external consultants who are called in to assist with an incident.

Regardless of the type of incident response, it is important to have a well-defined incident response plan in place to ensure a quick and effective response to a cyber security incident. This plan should outline the steps to be taken in the event of an incident, and should be regularly tested and updated to ensure its effectiveness.

In a nutshell

Incident response refers to the process of identifying and containing a cyber security incident, as well as the restoration of affected systems and data. There are three main types of incident response: proactive, reactive, and incident response teams.

It is important to have a well-defined incident response plan in place to ensure an effective response to a cyber security incident.

3. Digital forensics tools and techniques

Digital forensics involves the use of specialized tools and techniques to extract, preserve, and analyze digital data from a variety of sources, such as hard drives, smartphones, and cloud storage.

These tools and techniques are essential for ensuring the integrity and admissibility of the digital evidence.

In this chapter, we will explore the various tools and techniques used in digital forensics, including hardware and software tools, data acquisition and analysis, and network forensics.

We will also discuss the importance of following a systematic and methodical approach when using these tools and techniques to ensure the integrity and authenticity of the digital evidence.

Hardware and software tools

Hardware and software tools are essential for extracting, preserving, and analyzing digital data in a digital forensics investigation. These tools are used to collect and analyze digital evidence from a variety of sources, such as computers, servers, mobile devices, and cloud storage.

Hardware tools are physical devices used in digital forensics to extract and analyze digital data.

These tools may be used to acquire data from a variety of sources, including hard drives, mobile devices, and cloud storage.

Some common types of hardware tools used in digital forensics include:

- **Write blockers:** Write blockers are devices that prevent data from being written to a storage device during the forensic acquisition process. This helps to ensure the integrity and authenticity of the digital evidence[4].

  Some well-known products includes:

  - **Tableau TD2U**: A hardware-based write blocker[5] that supports a wide range of interfaces, including USB, SATA, SAS, and

---

[4] https://en.wikipedia.org/wiki/Forensic_disk_controller
[5] https://security.opentext.com/tableau/hardware/details/td2u

IDE. It is widely used in the DFIR community and is known for its reliability and compatibility with a wide range of devices.

- ○ **Forensic UltraDock FUDv6**: A hardware-based write blocker[6] that supports USB, SATA, and IDE interfaces. It is compact and portable, making it easy to use in a variety of situations.

- ○ **PC-3000 UDMA-E**: A hardware-based write blocker that supports SATA, SAS, and IDE interfaces[7].
  It is known for its advanced features and capabilities, including support for advanced data recovery and analysis.

- ○ **Belkasoft Evidence Center**: A software-based write blocker that supports a wide range of interfaces and devices[8]. It is known for its advanced features and capabilities, including support for forensic analysis and reporting.

- **Forensic imaging devices**: Forensic imaging

---

[6] https://wiebetech.com/products/forensic-ultradock-fudv6-0/
[7] https://www.acelab.eu.com/pc3000.udma.php
[8] https://belkasoft.com/x

devices are used to create a copy, or "forensic image," of a storage device. These devices may be hardware-based or software-based, and they are used to create an exact copy of the data on the storage device.

- **Physical analyzers**: Physical analyzers are used to analyze physical media, such as hard drives, for evidence of criminal activity or data breaches.

  These tools may be used to recover deleted or damaged data, or to identify patterns or anomalies in the data.

  Some suggestions:

  - **Chip-Off Forensics Kit**: A hardware-based physical analyzer[9] that allows for the examination and analysis of data stored on chips and integrated circuits. It is widely used in the DFIR community and is known for its reliability and compatibility with a wide range of devices.

  - **PC-3000 Flash**: A hardware-based physical analyzer[10] that allows for the examination and analysis of data stored on flash-based devices, such as USB drives and SSDs. It is

---

[9] https://cellebrite.com/
[10] https://www.acelab.eu.com/pc3000flash.php

known for its advanced features and capabilities, including support for advanced data recovery and analysis.

- ○ **Cellebrite Physical Analyzer**: A software-based physical analyzer[11] that allows for the examination and analysis of data stored on mobile devices, such as smartphones and tablets. It is known for its advanced features and capabilities, including support for forensic analysis and reporting.

- **JTAG/ISP** (In-System Programming) devices: JTAG/ISP[12] devices are used to extract data from embedded systems, such as those found in smartphones or Internet of Things (IoT) devices. These devices allow forensic analysts to access data that is not normally accessible through the user interface.

Some well-known products:

- ○ **JTAG Technologies**: A range of hardware-based JTAG/ISP tools[13] for the examination and analysis of data stored on chips and integrated circuits. These

---

[11] https://cellebrite.com/en/physical-analyzer/
[12] https://en.wikipedia.org/wiki/JTAG
[13] https://www.jtag.com/products/hardware/

> tools are widely used in the DFIR community and are known for their reliability and compatibility with a wide range of devices.

- ○ **Xeltek**: A range of hardware-based JTAG/ISP tools[14] for the examination and analysis of data stored on chips and integrated circuits. These tools are known for their advanced features and capabilities, including support for advanced data recovery and analysis.

Software tools are essential for extracting, preserving, and analyzing digital evidence in a digital forensics investigation.

Data acquisition tools are used to create a forensic copy of the digital evidence, often referred to as a *"forensic image."*

These tools allow the investigator to create a bit-by-bit copy of the digital evidence, ensuring the integrity and authenticity of the data.

Some common software tools used in digital forensics acquisition include:

- **OpenText EnCase Forensic**[15]: A popular data

---

[14] https://www.xeltek.com/isp-programmers/
[15] https://www.opentext.com/products/encase-forensic

acquisition and analysis tool used by law enforcement and forensic professionals.

- **FTK Imager**[16]: A data acquisition tool used to create forensic images of hard drives and other digital media.

- **X-Ways Forensics**[17]: A data acquisition and analysis tool used by forensic professionals.

It is important to choose the appropriate software tools for the specific needs of the investigation.

DFIR professionals should be familiar with a variety of software tools and know how to use them effectively to extract and analyze.

---

[16] https://www.exterro.com/ftk-imager
[17] https://www.x-ways.net/forensics/

Data analysis

Data analysis is a critical step in the digital forensics process.

It involves extracting relevant data and information from the digital evidence and creating a clear and concise report or testimony.

There are several key considerations when analyzing digital data:

- **Data analysis**: Data analysis involves extracting relevant data and information from the digital evidence and creating a clear and concise report or testimony.
  This may involve using specialized software tools to examine system logs, event logs, application data, and metadata. It is important to follow a systematic and methodical approach when analyzing digital data to ensure that the evidence is properly interpreted and presented.

- **Reporting**: The results of the data analysis should be presented in a clear and concise manner, often in the form of a report or testimony.
  This may involve visualizing the data, creating timelines, and presenting the findings in a way that is easily understood by the audience.

Some common software tools used for analysis and

reporting includes:

- **Autopsy**: An open source software-based tool[18] that allows for the analysis and reporting of data from a wide range of devices.
  It is widely used in the DFIR community and is known for its reliability and compatibility with a wide range of devices.

- **Sleuth Kit:** An open source software-based tool[19] that allows for the analysis and reporting of data from a wide range of devices.
  It is known for its advanced features and capabilities, including support for forensic analysis and reporting.

In a nutshell

Data acquisition and analysis are critical steps in the digital forensics process.

Data acquisition involves collecting and preserving digital evidence in a way that ensures its integrity and authenticity, while data analysis involves extracting relevant data and information from the digital evidence and creating a clear and concise report or testimony.

---

[18] https://www.autopsy.com/
[19] https://www.sleuthkit.org/

Network forensics

Network forensics involves the examination of network data for the purpose of identifying and investigating cyber security incidents or crimes.

It is a critical tool for law enforcement agencies, as well as companies and organizations looking to protect their assets and reputation.

Network forensics involves the collection and analysis of network data, including packets, logs, and other network artifacts.

This data may be collected from a variety of sources, such as firewalls, routers, switches, and servers.

There are several key considerations when conducting network forensics:

- **Data collection**: The first step in network forensics is to collect and preserve the relevant data. This may involve capturing network traffic, collecting system logs, or extracting data from devices and systems.
  It is important to follow a systematic and methodical approach when collecting data to ensure that the evidence is not contaminated or altered in any way.

- **Data analysis**: The next step in network forensics is to analyze the collected data to identify patterns, trends, and anomalies. This may involve using specialized software tools to examine packets, logs, and other network artifacts. It is important to follow a systematic and methodical approach when analyzing data to ensure that the evidence is properly interpreted and presented.

- **Reporting**: The results of the data analysis should be presented in a clear and concise manner, often in the form of a report or testimony. This may involve visualizing the data, creating timelines, and presenting the findings in a way that is easily understood by the audience.

Here are some examples of commercial, free, and open source products that may be useful for conducting network forensics:

Commercial:

- **Wireshark**: A powerful packet capture and analysis tool that is widely used in the DFIR community[20].

- **NetWitness**: A network security and analysis platform that offers a range of tools for capturing, analyzing, and visualizing network traffic[21].

- **Fluke Networks**: A range of network analysis and

---

[20] https://www.wireshark.org/

[21] https://www.netwitness.com/products/network-security-network-monitoring/

visualization tools[22], including network probes and analyzers.

Open source:

- **tcpdump**: A command-line packet capture and analysis tool that is widely used in the DFIR community.

- **Snort**: An open source intrusion detection and prevention system[23] that is widely used in the DFIR community.

- **SiLK**: A suite of tools for capturing, storing, and analyzing network traffic data[24].

- **Zeek**: An open source network analysis and security platform that offers[25] a range of tools for capturing, analyzing, and visualizing network traffic.

- **Suricata**: An open source network security platform[26] that offers a range of tools for capturing, analyzing, and visualizing network traffic.

---

[22] https://www.flukenetworks.com/installation-and-test
[23] https://www.snort.org/
[24] https://tools.netsa.cert.org/silk/
[25] https://zeek.org/
[26] https://suricata.io/

- **Ntop**: An open source network traffic analysis and visualization tool[27].

In a nutshell

Network forensics involves the examination of network data for the purpose of identifying and investigating cyber security incidents or crimes. It involves the collection and analysis of network data, including packets, logs, and other network artifacts, and the presentation of the results in a clear and concise manner.

---

[27] https://www.ntop.org/

4. Incident response process

Incident response refers to the process of identifying and containing a cyber security incident, as well as the restoration of affected systems and data. It is a proactive approach to prevent or minimize the impact of a cyber attack or data breach.

The incident response process typically involves four key steps: **preparation and planning, incident detection and triage, response and recovery**, and **post-incident analysis and reporting**.

In this chapter, we will explore each of these steps in detail, and discuss the importance of having a well-defined incident response plan in place to ensure a quick and effective response to a cyber security incident. We will also examine case studies and examples of real-world incident response scenarios and solutions.

Preparation and planning

Effective incident response requires proper preparation and planning to ensure that an organization is prepared to respond to a cyber security incident in a timely and effective manner.

Preparation and planning involve developing a comprehensive incident response plan that outlines the steps to be taken in the event of an incident.

An incident response plan should include:

- **A list of key stakeholders** and their roles and responsibilities in the incident response process. This may include IT staff, management, legal counsel, and external consultants or contractors.

- **A clear and concise communication plan**, including protocols for internal and external communication. This may include a list of contact information for key stakeholders, as well as guidelines for communicating with customers, employees, and the media.

- **Guidelines** for identifying and triaging incidents. This may include procedures for detecting an incident, determining its severity, and escalating it to the appropriate stakeholders.

- **Procedures** for responding to and recovering from

incidents. This may include steps for containing the incident, restoring affected systems and data, and mitigating the impact.

- Guidelines for **post-incident analysis and reporting**. This may include procedures for conducting a root cause analysis, preparing a post-incident report, and implementing corrective actions to prevent future incidents.

It is important to regularly test and update the incident response plan to ensure its effectiveness.

This may involve conducting tabletop exercises or simulated incidents to identify any weaknesses or gaps in the plan.

In a nutshell

Effective incident response requires proper preparation and planning to ensure that an organization is prepared to respond to a cyber security incident in a timely and effective manner.

A well-defined incident response plan should include a list of key stakeholders, a communication plan, guidelines for identifying and triaging incidents, procedures for responding to and recovering from incidents, and guidelines

Incident detection and triage

Incident detection and triage are critical steps in the incident response process. Incident detection involves identifying and verifying that an incident has occurred, while incident triage involves determining the severity of the incident and escalating it to the appropriate stakeholders.

There are several key considerations when detecting and triaging incidents:

- **Detection**: Incident detection involves identifying and verifying that an incident has occurred. This may involve monitoring system logs, network traffic, and security alerts, as well as receiving reports from employees or customers. It is important to have a robust incident detection system in place to ensure that incidents are identified and reported in a timely manner.

- **Triage**: Incident triage involves determining the severity of the incident and escalating it to the appropriate stakeholders. This may involve determining the extent of the damage, the potential impact on business operations, and the likelihood of future incidents. It is important to have a clear and concise process in place for triaging incidents to ensure that they are properly prioritized and addressed.

- **Communication**: Effective communication is critical to the success of the incident response process. It is important to have a clear and concise communication plan in place to ensure that all stakeholders are informed and involved in the response and recovery process.

In a nutshell

Incident detection and triage are critical steps in the incident response process. Incident detection involves identifying and verifying that an incident has occurred, while incident triage involves determining the severity of the incident and escalating it to the appropriate stakeholders.

Effective communication is also critical to the success of the incident response process.

Response and recovery

Response and recovery are critical steps in the incident response process. Response involves containing the incident and mitigating the impact, while recovery involves restoring affected systems and data.

There are several key considerations when responding to and recovering from an incident:

- **Containment**: The first step in response is to contain the incident to prevent further damage or disruption. This may involve disconnecting affected systems from the network, disabling compromised accounts, or implementing other measures to prevent the spread of the incident.

- **Mitigation**: The next step in response is to mitigate the impact of the incident. This may involve identifying and repairing any damage, implementing measures to prevent future incidents, and communicating with stakeholders about the incident and the steps being taken to address it.

- **Recovery**: Recovery involves restoring affected systems and data to their pre-incident state. This may involve repairing or replacing damaged hardware, restoring data from backups, and testing systems to ensure that they are functioning correctly.

- **Communication**: Effective communication is critical to the success of the incident response process. It is important to keep stakeholders informed about the progress of the response and recovery efforts, and to communicate any actions that may be necessary to prevent future incidents.

Post-incident analysis and reporting

Post-incident analysis and reporting are important steps in the incident response process, as they help to identify the root cause of the incident and implement corrective actions to prevent future incidents.

There are several key considerations when conducting post-incident analysis and reporting:

- **Root cause analysis**: A root cause analysis is a systematic process for identifying the underlying cause of an incident. This may involve reviewing system logs, network traffic, and other data, as well as conducting interviews with relevant stakeholders. The goal of the root cause analysis is to identify the root cause of the incident and implement corrective actions to prevent future incidents.

- **Post-incident report**: A post-incident report is a detailed document that outlines the events leading up to the incident, the actions taken to respond and recover, and the results of the root cause analysis. The post-incident report should be clear and concise, and should include recommendations for improving incident response processes and procedures.

- **Corrective actions**: Corrective actions are measures taken to prevent future incidents from occurring. These may include implementing new security measures, training employees on cyber security best practices, and conducting regular security assessments.

- **Communication**: Effective communication is critical to the success of the incident response process. It is important to keep stakeholders informed about the progress of the post-incident analysis and reporting efforts, and to communicate any corrective actions that may be necessary to prevent future incidents.

There are different methodologies that can be applied to the creation of a post-incident report, but I think the best documentation on this is that provided by the **Australian Cyber Security Centre**, which has published a set of guidelines and templates dedicated to incident response issues.

In fact, in *Chapter 14.1* of its **Cyber Incident Response Plan**[28], *ACSC* provides a set of guidelines for creating a Post Incident Review document:

> A Post Incident Review (PIR) is a detailed review conducted after an organisation has experienced a

---

[28] https://www.cyber.gov.au/acsc/view-all-content/publications/cyber-incident-response-plan

cyber security incident. It can include a hot debrief which is held immediately after an organisation has recovered its networks and systems from a cyber security incident and a formal debrief held after the incident report has been completed, such as within two weeks.

Key questions to consider in your PIR:

- What were the root causes of the incident and any incident response issues?
- Could the incident have been prevented? How?
- What worked well in the response to the incident?
- How can our response be improved for future incidents?

In the appendix, ACSC also provides more details about the process along with a convenient template that can be used to produce the report.

In a nutshell

In summary, post-incident analysis and reporting are important steps in the incident response process, as they help to identify the root cause of the incident and implement corrective actions to prevent future incidents.

A post-incident report should be clear and concise, and

should include recommendations for improving incident response processes and procedures.

5. Legal considerations in DFIR

Digital forensics and incident response (DFIR) often intersect with legal issues, particularly when the digital evidence is being used in a criminal or civil proceeding.

It is important for DFIR professionals to have a solid understanding of the legal considerations involved in the collection, preservation, and analysis of digital evidence.

In this chapter, we will explore the legal issues involved in DFIR, including the admissibility and authenticity of digital evidence, the role of expert testimony, and the ethical considerations of conducting digital forensics. We will also discuss the legal framework for DFIR, including relevant laws, regulations, and guidelines.

Admissibility of digital evidence in court

The admissibility of digital evidence in court is a critical consideration in DFIR. Digital evidence must meet certain legal standards in order to be admitted as evidence in a criminal or civil proceeding.

These standards include relevance, authenticity, and reliability.

- **Relevance**: Digital evidence must be relevant to the case in order to be admissible. This means that the evidence must have a direct bearing on the issues at hand and be material to the case.

- **Authenticity**: Digital evidence must be authentic in order to be admissible. This means that it must be genuine and not altered or tampered with in any way. In order to establish authenticity, it may be necessary to provide a chain of custody for the evidence, as well as testify to the methods used to collect and preserve the evidence.

- **Reliability**: Digital evidence must be reliable in order to be admissible. This means that it must be accurate and dependable, and not subject to error or distortion. In order to establish reliability, it may be necessary to provide expert testimony or to demonstrate the accuracy and reliability of the methods used to collect and analyze the evidence.

It is important for DFIR professionals to be aware of these legal standards and to follow a systematic and methodical approach when collecting, preserving, and analyzing digital evidence to ensure its admissibility in court.

In a nutshell

In summary, the admissibility of digital evidence in court is a critical consideration in DFIR. Digital evidence must be relevant, authentic, and reliable in order to be admitted as evidence in a criminal or civil proceeding. It is important for DFIR professionals to be aware

Ethical considerations

Ethical considerations are an important aspect of DFIR, as they pertain to the moral principles and values that guide the conduct of professionals in the field. DFIR professionals are expected to adhere to a high standard of ethics in the collection, preservation, and analysis of digital evidence.

There are several key ethical considerations in DFIR:

- **Professionalism**: DFIR professionals are expected to conduct themselves in a professional manner, including acting with integrity, honesty, and respect for the law and the rights of others.

- **Confidentiality**: DFIR professionals are often entrusted with sensitive and confidential information. It is important to maintain the confidentiality of this information and to protect the privacy of individuals whose data is being analyzed.

- **Objectivity**: DFIR professionals are expected to be objective and unbiased in the collection and analysis of digital evidence.
  This means avoiding any conflicts of interest and conducting the analysis in an impartial and objective manner.

- **Expert testimony**: DFIR professionals may be

called upon to provide expert testimony in a legal proceeding. It is important to be honest and accurate in providing testimony, and to disclose any potential biases or limitations in the analysis.

In a nutshell

Ethical considerations are an important aspect of DFIR. DFIR professionals are expected to adhere to a high standard of ethics in the collection, preservation, and analysis of digital evidence, including acting with professionalism, confidentiality, objectivity, and honesty.

6. Advanced topics in DFIR

DFIR is a rapidly evolving field that covers a wide range of topics and techniques. In this chapter, we will explore some of the more advanced topics in DFIR, including mobile device forensics, cloud forensics, and forensic analysis of big data.

- **Mobile device forensics**: Mobile devices, such as smartphones and tablets, are increasingly being used to store and transmit sensitive data. Mobile device forensics involves the collection, preservation, and analysis of data from these devices for the purpose of investigating cyber security incidents or crimes.

- **Cloud forensics**: Cloud computing has become increasingly popular in recent years, with many organizations outsourcing the storage and processing of their data to cloud service providers. Cloud forensics involves the examination of data stored in the cloud for the purpose of identifying and investigating cyber security incidents or crimes.

- **Forensic analysis of big data**: Big data refers to large and complex data sets that may be difficult to process using traditional data processing techniques. Forensic analysis of big data involves the examination of these data sets for the purpose of identifying and investigating cyber security incidents or crimes.

This chapter explores some of the more advanced topics in DFIR, including mobile device forensics, cloud forensics, and forensic analysis of big data.

Mobile device forensics

Mobile device forensics involves the collection, preservation, and analysis of data from mobile devices, such as smartphones and tablets, for the purpose of investigating cyber security incidents or crimes.

Mobile devices are increasingly being used to store and transmit sensitive data, making them an important source of digital evidence in DFIR.

There are several key considerations in mobile device forensics:

- **Collection**: The first step in mobile device forensics is to collect the data from the device. This may involve physically acquiring the device, or accessing the data remotely through a network connection. It is important to follow a systematic and methodical approach to ensure the integrity and authenticity of the data.
  This may involve using specialized hardware and software tools to acquire the data, as well as following established protocols for handling the device.

- **Preservation**: The next step in mobile device forensics is to preserve the data in its original form. This may involve creating a forensic image of the device, or extracting specific data elements. It is important to follow industry best practices and guidelines to ensure that the data is preserved in a manner that is legally admissible. This may involve using hashing algorithms to verify the integrity of the data, as well as following established protocols for storing and handling the data.

- **Analysis**: The final step in mobile device forensics is to analyze the data to identify any relevant evidence. This may involve using specialized software tools to examine the data, as well as conducting manual analysis to identify patterns or anomalies. It is important to follow a systematic and methodical approach to ensure that all relevant evidence is identified and analyzed. This may involve using a structured approach to analyze the data, such as the CARVER methodology, as well as following established guidelines for analyzing specific types of data, such as call logs or text messages.

One important aspect of mobile device forensics is extracting data from the device.

There are several methods for extracting data from mobile devices:

- **Physical acquisition**: Physical acquisition involves physically acquiring the device and extracting the data from it. This may involve using specialized hardware and software tools to connect to the device and extract the data, or physically disassembling the device and extracting the data from the memory chips. Physical acquisition is often the preferred method, as it allows for the extraction of the most comprehensive and comprehensive set of data.

- **Logical acquisition**: Logical acquisition involves accessing the data remotely through a network connection. This may involve using specialized software tools to connect to the device and extract the data, or using a cloud-based service to access the data. Logical acquisition is often more convenient and faster than physical acquisition, but it may not be as comprehensive.

- **Data extraction from backups:** Another method for extracting data from mobile devices is to extract it from backups. Many mobile devices automatically create backups of their data, which can be accessed and extracted using specialized software tools. This is often a useful method for extracting data from devices that are damaged or otherwise inaccessible.

Here are some examples of commercial and free products that may be useful for mobile device forensics:

- **Cellebrite UFED:** A commercial software-based tool[29] that allows for the extraction and analysis of

---

[29] https://cellebrite.com/en/ufed-ultimate/

data from a wide range of mobile devices, including smartphones and tablets. It is widely used in the DFIR community and is known for its reliability and compatibility with a wide range of devices.

- **Oxygen Forensic Detective**: A commercial software-based suite[30] that allows for the extraction and analysis of data from a wide range of mobile devices, including smartphones and tablets. It is known for its advanced features and capabilities, including support for forensic analysis and reporting.

- **Mobile Forensic Toolkit (MFTK)**: An open source software-based tool that allows for the extraction and analysis of data from a wide range of mobile devices, including smartphones and tablets[31]. It is known for its advanced features and capabilities, including support for forensic analysis and reporting.

---

[30] https://www.oxygen-forensic.com/en/products/oxygen-forensic-detective
[31] https://www.exterro.com/forensic-toolkit

Cloud forensics

Cloud forensics involves the examination of data stored in the cloud for the purpose of identifying and investigating cyber security incidents or crimes. One important aspect of cloud forensics is extracting data from the cloud.

There are several methods for extracting data from the cloud:

- **Direct access:** One method for extracting data from the cloud is to access it directly through the cloud provider's API. This requires obtaining the appropriate credentials and following the cloud provider's guidelines for accessing the data.

- **Data dumps**: Another method for extracting data from the cloud is to request a data dump from the cloud provider.
This involves requesting all the data stored in the cloud in a specific format, such as a CSV file. Data dumps can be useful for extracting large amounts of data, but they may not be as comprehensive as other methods.

- **Third-party tools**: There are also a number of third-party tools available for extracting data from the cloud. These tools may offer a more comprehensive and customizable solution for extracting data, but they may also be more expensive and require more technical expertise to use.

The most comprehensive and customizable solution for extracting data is often through the use of third-party tools, but other methods may be more convenient or faster.

Some examples of commercial and products products that may be useful for conducting cloud forensics includes:

- **BlackBag Cloud Forensics:** A commercial[32] software-based tool that allows for the extraction and analysis of data from cloud-based storage and services. It is known for its advanced features and capabilities, including support for forensic analysis and reporting.

- **Magnet AXIOM:** A commercial software-based tool[33] that allows for the extraction and analysis of data from cloud-based storage and services. It is known for its advanced features and capabilities, including support for forensic analysis and reporting.

- **Cloud Forensic Utils:** A free software-based tool that allows for the extraction and analysis of data

---

[32] https://cellebrite.com/en/cellebrite-blackbag-advantage/
[33] https://www.magnetforensics.com/products/magnet-axiom/

from cloud-based storage and services[34].

---

[34] https://github.com/google/cloud-forensics-utils

Malware analysis

Malware analysis is a key aspect of DFIR, as it involves the examination of malicious software (malware) for the purpose of identifying and understanding its capabilities and behaviors.

Malware is often used in cyber attacks to compromise systems and steal sensitive data, making it an important area of focus for DFIR professionals.

There are several key considerations in malware analysis:

- **Static analysis**: Static analysis involves examining the code and structure of the malware without executing it. This may involve using specialized software tools to disassemble or decompile the malware, or manually analyzing the code to identify key features and functions. Static analysis can provide valuable information about the malware's capabilities and behaviors, but it may not reveal all of its secrets.

- **Dynamic analysis**: Dynamic analysis involves executing the malware in a controlled environment, or sandbox, to observe its behaviors and effects. This may involve using specialized software tools to monitor the malware's activities, or manually observing its behavior. Dynamic analysis can provide valuable insights into the malware's capabilities and behaviors, but it can also be risky, as the malware may attempt to compromise the sandbox or perform malicious actions.

- **Reverse engineering**: Reverse engineering involves deconstructing the malware to understand its inner workings. This may involve using specialized software tools to decompile the malware, or manually analyzing the code to identify key functions and behaviors. Reverse engineering can provide valuable insights into the malware's capabilities and behaviors, but it can also be time-consuming and require advanced technical skills.

Below a brief list of commercial and open source products that may be useful for conducting malware analysis and reverse engineering:

- **IDA Pro:** A commercial tool[35] that allows for the analysis and reverse engineering of software, including malware. It is widely used in the DFIR community and is known for its advanced features and capabilities.

- **OllyDbg**: A free tool[36] that allows for the analysis and reverse engineering of software, including

---

[35] https://www.hex-rays.com/ida-pro/
[36] https://www.ollydbg.de/

malware. It is widely used in the DFIR community and is known for its advanced features and capabilities.

- **Hiew:** A commercial software[37] that allows for the analysis and reverse engineering of software, including malware. It is known for its advanced features and capabilities, including support for advanced data recovery and analysis.

- **Binary Ninja:** A commercial tool that allows[38] for the analysis and reverse engineering of software, including malware. It is known for its advanced features and capabilities, including support for advanced data recovery and analysis.

- **Ghidra:** An open source software that allows for the analysis and reverse engineering of software, including malware[39]. It is widely used in the DFIR community and is known for its advanced features and capabilities.

- **Volatility:** An open source software-based tool that allows for the analysis and identification of malware[40]. It is widely used in the DFIR community and is known for its reliability and

---

[37] https://www.hiew.ru/
[38] https://binary.ninja/
[39] https://ghidra-sre.org/
[40] https://www.volatilityfoundation.org/

compatibility with a wide range of devices.

- **Yara:** An open source software-based tool that allows for the analysis and identification of malware[41]. It is known for its advanced features and capabilities, including support for forensic analysis and reporting.

In a nutshell

Malware analysis can provide valuable insights into the malware's capabilities and behaviors.
However, each approach has its own benefits and risks, and it is important to follow established best practices and guidelines when conducting malware analysis.

---

[41] https://github.com/VirusTotal/yara

7. Case studies and examples

Case studies and examples are a useful way to illustrate the principles and techniques of DFIR in action.

In this chapter, we will present several case studies and examples to demonstrate the practical application of DFIR in real-world scenarios.

Case study 1: Malware analysis

Scenario: A large financial institution has experienced a cyber attack, with the attackers deploying malware on their systems.

The institution has hired a DFIR team to investigate the attack and determine the extent of the damage.

Objectives:

- Identify the type of malware that was used in the attack and its intended purpose.
- Analyze the malware to determine its capabilities and functions, including any malicious actions it may have taken.
- Determine the extent of the malware's spread within the organization's systems and identify any potentially affected data or systems.
- Develop a plan to remove the malware and secure the systems against future attacks.
- Analyze any potential indicators of compromise (IOCs) to identify the attackers and their methods of operation.

In this case study, the DFIR team would need to utilize tools and techniques for malware analysis and reverse engineering to thoroughly analyze the malware and its impact on the organization's systems. This may include using tools such as IDA Pro or Ghidra to disassemble and analyze the malware code, and utilizing network forensics and traffic analysis to identify any potential IOCs or patterns of behavior.

Additionally, the team may need to work closely with the organization's IT and security staff to implement the necessary security measures and protocols to prevent future attacks.

Case study 2: Network forensics

Scenario: A medium-sized e-commerce company has experienced a cyber attack, with the attackers gaining unauthorized access to the company's systems and customer data. The company has hired a DFIR team to investigate the attack and determine the extent of the damage.

Objectives:

- Identify the cause of the breach and the method used by the attackers to gain access to the systems.
- Determine the extent of the data breach and the types of data that were accessed or compromised.
- Analyze network traffic and logs to identify any potential indicators of compromise (IOCs) and patterns of behavior.
- Identify any vulnerabilities or weaknesses in the company's systems that may have contributed to the breach.
- Develop a plan to secure the systems and prevent future attacks.

In this case study, the DFIR team would need to utilize tools and techniques for network forensics to thoroughly analyze the network traffic and logs in order to identify any potential IOCs or patterns of behavior.

This may include using tools such as Wireshark or NetWitness Investigator to analyze network traffic, and utilizing log analysis tools such as Splunk or LogRhythm to identify any suspicious activity.

Case study 3: Cybercrime Investigation

Scenario: A small business has experienced a cyber attack, with the attackers gaining access to sensitive financial data and customer information. The business owner has contacted law enforcement and hired a DFIR team to investigate the breach and determine the extent of the damage.

Objectives:

- Identify the cause of the breach and the method used by the attackers to gain access to the systems.
- Determine the extent of the data breach and the types of data that were accessed or compromised.
- Identify any vulnerabilities or weaknesses in the business's systems that may have contributed to the breach.
- Develop a plan to secure the systems and prevent future attacks.

Case study 4: Insider Threat Investigation

Scenario: A large corporation has received a tip from an anonymous source that an employee is engaging in unethical or illegal activities using company resources. The corporation has hired a DFIR team to investigate the allegations and determine the truth.

Objectives:

- Identify the employee in question and the specific activities they are alleged to have engaged in.
- Gather and analyze digital evidence to confirm or refute the allegations.
- Determine the extent of the employee's access to company resources and systems, and identify any potential vulnerabilities or risks.
- Develop a plan to address the situation and prevent future insider threats.

Case study 5: Data Breach Response

Scenario: A large healthcare organization has experienced a data breach, with the attackers gaining access to sensitive patient data. The organization has hired a DFIR team to investigate the breach and implement a response plan.

Objectives:

- Identify the cause of the breach and the method used by the attackers to gain access to the systems.
- Determine the extent of the data breach and the types of data that were accessed or compromised.
- Identify any vulnerabilities or weaknesses in the organization's systems that may have contributed to the breach.
- Develop and implement a plan to secure the systems and prevent future attacks.
- Communicate with affected parties, including patients, employees, and regulatory bodies, to ensure that all necessary steps are taken to protect the data and minimize any potential impact.

Case study 6: Ransomware attack

Scenario: A large healthcare organization has experienced a ransomware attack, with the attackers encrypting the organization's data and demanding a ransom for the decryption key. The organization has hired a DFIR team to investigate the attack and determine the best course of action.

Objectives:

- Identify the type of ransomware that was used in the attack and its intended purpose.
- Determine the extent of the ransomware's spread within the organization's systems and identify any potentially affected data or systems.
- Analyze the ransom demand and any associated communications with the attackers to determine the likelihood of receiving a valid decryption key.
- Develop a plan to respond to the ransomware attack, including determining whether to pay the ransom, attempting to restore from backups, or seeking alternative solutions.
- Communicate with affected parties, including patients, employees, and regulatory bodies, to ensure that all necessary steps are taken to protect the data and minimize any potential impact.

In this real-world scenario, the DFIR team would need to quickly assess the situation and determine the best course of action in response to the ransomware attack.

This may involve analyzing the ransom demand and any associated communications with the attackers to determine the likelihood of receiving a valid decryption key, and weighing the potential risks and costs associated with paying the ransom versus attempting to restore from backups or seeking alternative solutions.

The team may also need to work closely with the organization's IT and security staff to implement the necessary security measures and protocols to prevent future attacks.

Case study 7: Phishing Attack

Scenario: A medium-sized non-profit organization has experienced a phishing attack, with the attackers gaining access to sensitive employee and donor data. The organization has hired a DFIR team to investigate the attack and determine the extent of the damage.

Objectives:

- Identify the cause of the attack and the method used by the attackers to gain access to the systems.
- Determine the extent of the data breach and the types of data that were accessed or compromised.
- Analyze email and web traffic to identify any potential indicators of compromise (IOCs) and patterns of behavior.
- Identify any vulnerabilities or weaknesses in the organization's systems that may have contributed to the attack.
- Develop a plan to secure the systems and prevent future attacks.

Case study 8: Malware Attack

Scenario: A large government agency has experienced a malware attack, with the attackers deploying malware on their systems. The agency has hired a DFIR team to investigate the attack and determine the extent of the damage.

Objectives:

- Identify the type of malware that was used in the attack and its intended purpose.
- Analyze the malware to determine its capabilities and functions, including any malicious actions it may have taken.
- Determine the extent of the malware's spread within the agency's systems and identify any potentially affected data or systems.
- Develop a plan to remove the malware and secure the systems against future attacks.
- Analyze any potential IOCs to identify the attackers and their methods of operation.

Case study 9: Denial of Service (DoS) Attack

Scenario: A medium-sized e-commerce company has experienced a denial of service (DoS) attack, with the attackers flooding the company's website with traffic in an attempt to bring it down. The company has hired a DFIR team to investigate the attack and determine the best course of action.

Objectives:

- Identify the cause of the attack and the method used by the attackers to flood the website with traffic.
- Determine the extent of the attack and its impact on the company's website and systems.
- Identify any vulnerabilities or weaknesses in the company's systems that may have contributed to the attack.
- Develop a plan to defend against future DoS attacks, including implementing security measures such as firewalls and intrusion prevention systems.
- Communicate with affected parties, including customers and employees, to ensure that all necessary steps are taken to minimize any potential impact.

Case study 10: Social Engineering Attack

Scenario: A large financial institution has experienced a social engineering attack, with the attackers using various tactics such as phishing or pretexting to gain access to sensitive data. The institution has hired a DFIR team to investigate the attack and determine the extent of the damage.

Objectives:

- Identify the cause of the attack and the method used by the attackers to gain access to the data.
- Determine the extent of the data breach and the types of data that were accessed or compromised.
- Analyze email and web traffic to identify any potential indicators of compromise (IOCs) and patterns of behavior.
- Identify any vulnerabilities or weaknesses in the institution's systems or employee training that may have contributed to the attack.
- Develop a plan to secure the systems and prevent future attacks, including implementing stronger security measures and training employees on how to identify and prevent social engineering attacks.

8. Conclusion

In this book, we have explored the fundamental concepts and techniques of DFIR, as well as the tools and techniques used by DFIR professionals.

In this concluding chapter, we will summarize the key points covered in the book and offer some final thoughts on the importance of DFIR in today's digital age.

We will also discuss some of the challenges and opportunities facing DFIR professionals in the future, and provide some guidance on how to succeed in this exciting and dynamic field.

Summary of key points

In this book, we have explored the fundamental concepts and techniques of digital forensics and incident response (DFIR).

Here are some of the key points covered:

- DFIR is the process of identifying, analyzing, and responding to cyber security incidents or crimes. **It involves the collection, preservation, and analysis of digital evidence to identify and understand the** source and extent of an incident, and to identify and mitigate any potential risks or impacts.

- **DFIR professionals use a wide range of tools and techniques to conduct investigations,** including hardware and software tools, data acquisition and analysis techniques, network forensics techniques, and incident response processes.

- **Mobile device forensics involves the collection, preservation, and analysis of data from mobile devices,** such as smartphones and tablets. It is an important aspect of DFIR, as mobile devices are increasingly being used to store and transmit sensitive data.

- **Cloud forensics involves the examination of data stored in the cloud** for the purpose of identifying and investigating cyber security incidents or crimes. It requires careful consideration of legal and ethical guidelines when accessing the data, and the use of industry best practices and guidelines to ensure that the data is preserved in a manner that is legally admissible.

- **Malware analysis involves the examination of malicious software (malware) for the purpose of identifying and understanding its capabilities and behaviors.** It may involve static analysis, dynamic analysis, or reverse engineering, and can provide valuable insights into the malware's capabilities and behaviors.

- **DFIR professionals are often called upon to respond to a wide range of cyber security incidents and crimes.** These may include malware attacks, data breaches, or other cyber threats. It is important to follow a systematic and methodical approach to ensure that all relevant evidence is collected and analyzed, and to follow established best practices and guidelines to ensure the integrity and authenticity of the data.

DFIR is a critical discipline that plays a vital role in protecting organizations from cyber security threats and incidents. It involves the use of a wide range of tools and techniques to identify, analyze, and respond to cyber security incidents or crimes.

Future directions in DFIR

Digital forensics and incident response (DFIR) is a dynamic and rapidly evolving field, and it is likely to continue to evolve in the coming years as new technologies and threats emerge. Here are some of the key trends and challenges that DFIR professionals may face in the future:

- **Increasing complexity of cyber threats:** Cyber threats are becoming increasingly sophisticated and persistent, with Advanced Persistent Threats (APTs) and other complex threats becoming more common. DFIR professionals will need to continue to develop new and innovative techniques to identify and respond to these threats.

- **Rising demand for DFIR skills:** As cyber threats continue to evolve, there will be a growing demand for DFIR professionals with the skills and expertise to identify and respond to these threats. This will create new opportunities for DFIR professionals, as well as challenges in terms of competition and demand for specialized skills.

- **Growing importance of cloud and mobile forensics:** The increasing adoption of cloud computing and the proliferation of mobile devices are likely to drive the growth of cloud and mobile forensics as key areas of focus for DFIR professionals.

These areas will require specialized skills and expertise, as well as a deep understanding of the legal and ethical considerations involved.

- **Emerging technologies and platforms:** New technologies and platforms, such as the Internet of Things (IoT) and artificial intelligence (AI), are likely to present new challenges and opportunities for DFIR professionals.
These technologies may require specialized skills and expertise to identify and respond to cyber security incidents, and may also present new legal and ethical considerations.

In conclusion, DFIR is a dynamic and rapidly evolving field that is likely to continue to evolve in the coming years. DFIR professionals will need to stay up-to-date with the latest trends and technologies, and continue to develop new and innovative techniques to identify and respond to cyber threats.

ABOUT THE AUTHOR

I have been working in information technology since before the "Millennium Bug" and have been interested in cybersecurity since before the term cybersecurity was first used.